This book is dedicated to all the mothers out there.

What a gift to have, the gift of life.

I would also like to dedicate this book to my own mother.

She taught me
to question,
to explore,
to giggle,
to volunteer,
to support others,
to never give up,
to enjoy the journey,
to fail gracefully,
to succeed gracefully,
to love deeply.

I admire her so.

Illustrations copyright (c) 2013 Jean Gray Mohs

All rights reserved. No part of this publication may be reproduced or transmitted in any form or by any means, electronic or mechanical, including photocopy, recording, or any information storage and retrieval system, without permission in writing from the publisher.

The text of this book is set in Tallys.

First Edition

Mamalu's Secrets
Letters between mother and daughter

Written and Illustrated by Jean Gray Mohs
& her mother Ellen Drake

My Four Dots Publishing
www.myfourdots.com

Hello Mamalu!!
How are you?
I am fine and happy too!
Love you, Jeanniebu

Dearest Jeannie,
You've made my day,
with this letter
covered in happy spray.

This is Momma's secret you know.
Sneak into your bedroom when you're fast asle
and spray just a bit of happiness
so you will keep.

Dear Mamalu,
Is that why I turned out so good?
Because of the spray or because
of your motherhood?

You turned out so great
for many reasons,
good solid upbringing,
laughter through the seasons.

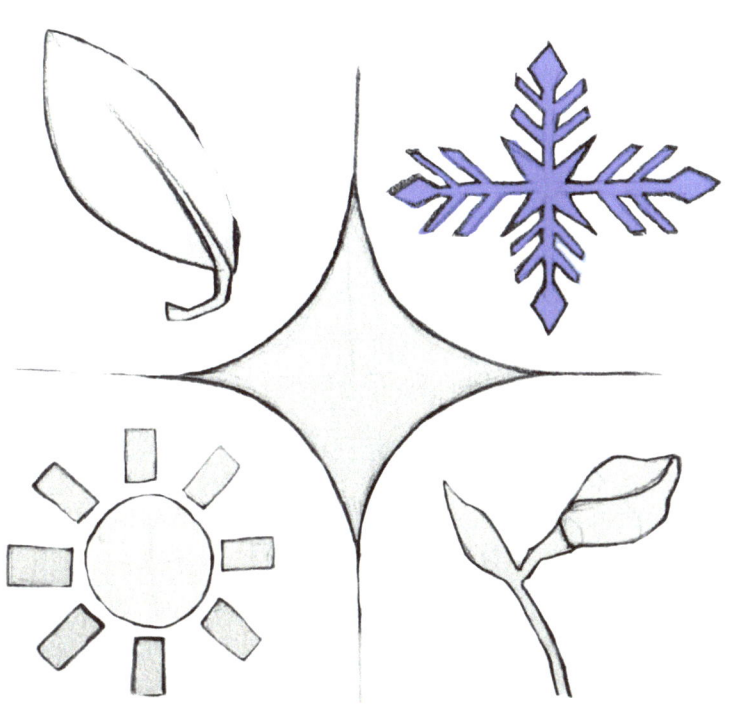

Bits of me, bits of dad
sprinkled from above,
a whole lot of family
and some brotherly love.

A big ol' box of crayons
museums, books and plays
a comfortable house
and lots of lighthearted days.

Some incredible friends
who saw you through
when it got too rough and your heart was
dark blue.

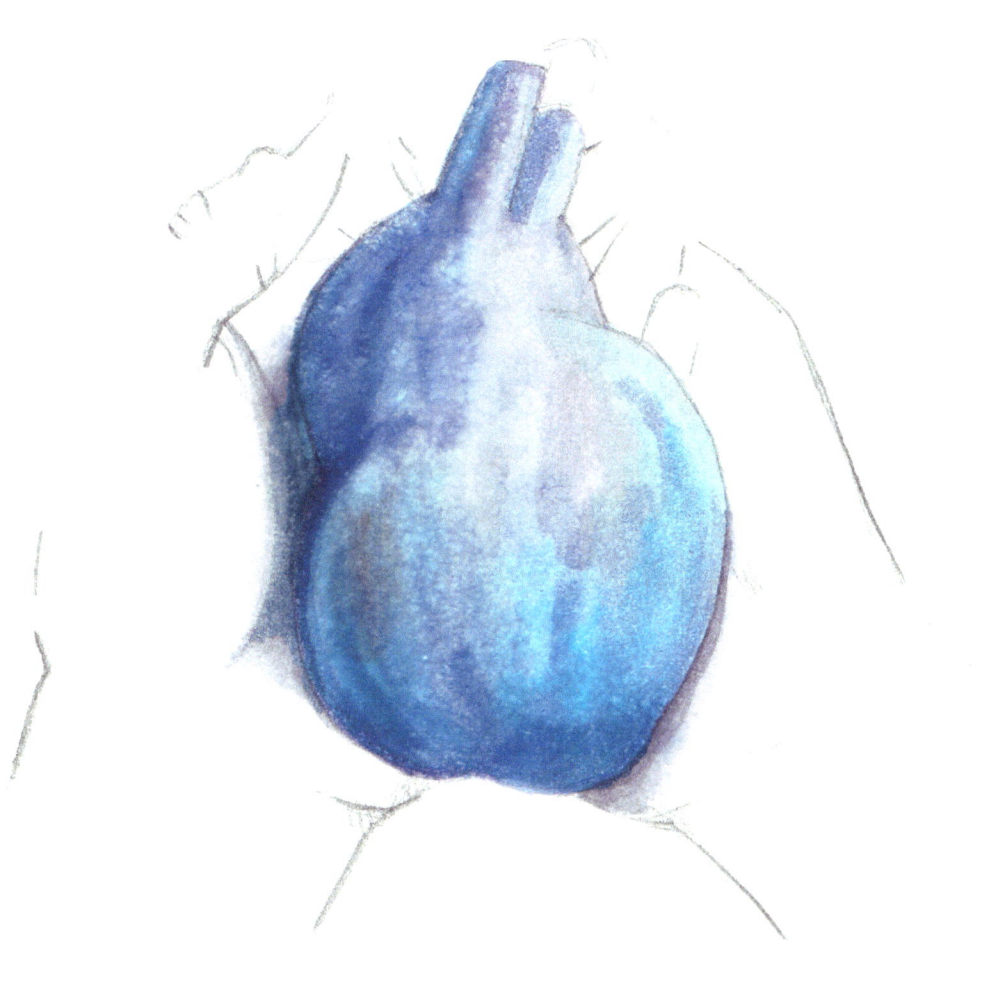

And some terrific adventures,
rugged mountains climbed,
lots of cats to hold,
lots of songs that rhymed.

We only get some credit,
the rest was up to you.
what to make with all your blessings
what to be, what to do

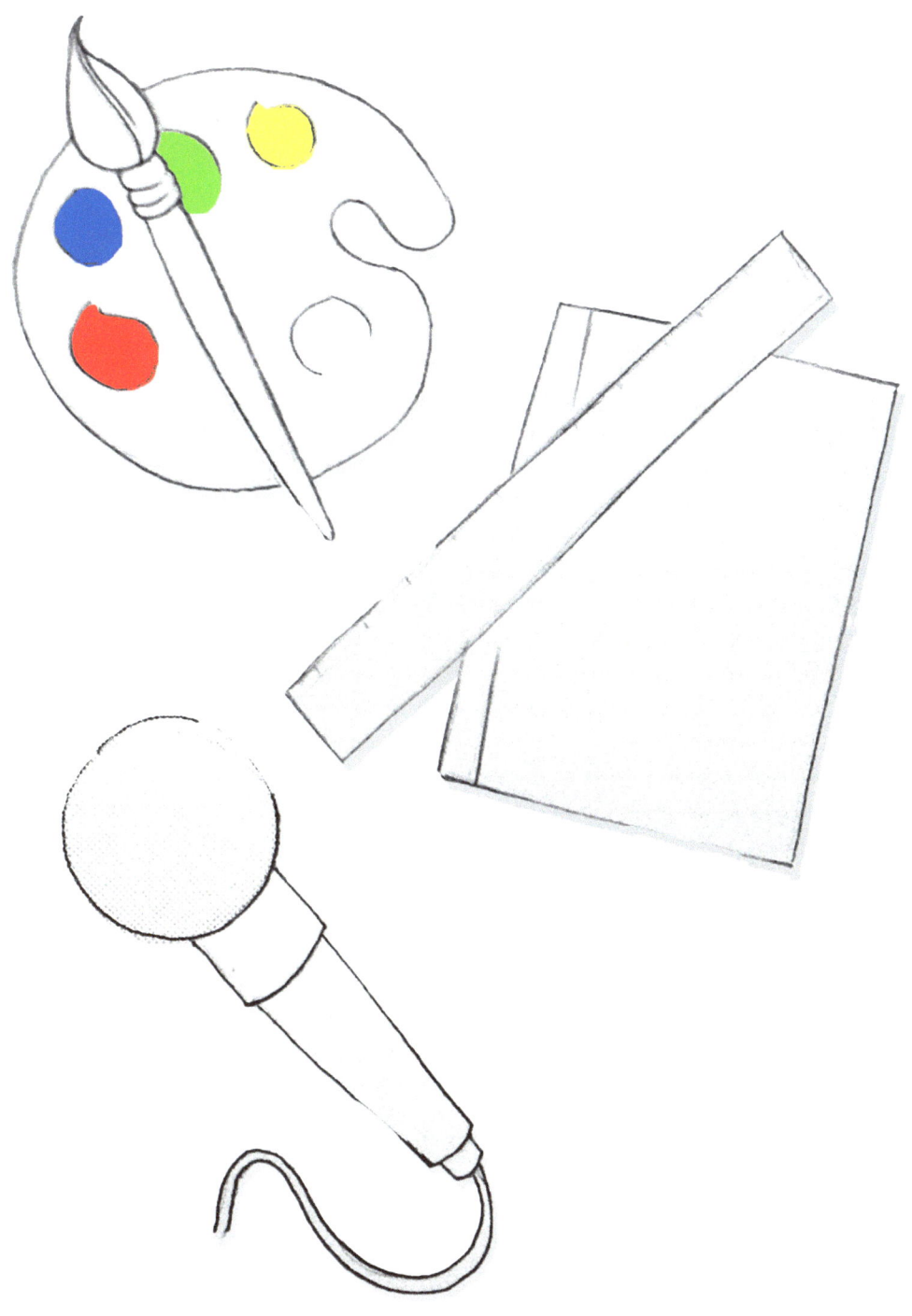

So you took them and shook them
sometimes giving us a fright,
and you made a Jeanniebu mixture
that brings us joy both day and night

I may have took them and shook them
but you gave me the tools.
Like you said a bit of dad and a bit of you
you gave us life's rules.

Dad likes weather, tennis and songs
drawing out maps and finding things lost.
You like math and morphing clay
seeking out culture at whatever cost.

$1 + 1 = 2$

You are the one that drove me there
museums, zoos, plays, everywhere.
Spending your hours to make our life full
you are the one that is rare.

Always cheering us along
making us feel amazing.
Art lessons, music lessons
your love so bright it was blazing.

Mom it was I,
being born to you two,
who was the lucky one.
The thanks belongs to you.

www.ingramcontent.com/pod-product-compliance
Lightning Source LLC
Chambersburg PA
CBHW041308110426
42743CB00037B/38